PRODUCERS, CONSUMERS, AND DECOMPOSERS

DAVA PRESSBERG

NEW YORK

Published in 2017 by The Rosen Publishing Group, Inc.
29 East 21st Street, New York, NY 10010

Editor: Caitie McAneney
Book Design: Michael Flynn
Interior Layout: Tanya Dellaccio

Photo Credits: Cover Eduard Kyslynskyy/Shutterstock.com; p. 4 (flowers) Madlen/Shutterstock.com; p. 4 (bee) irin-k/ Shutterstock.com; p. 4 (bird) Super Prin/Shutterstock.com; p. 4 (worm) Valentina Razumova/Shutterstock.com; p. 5 Ikordela/Shutterstock.com; p. 7 wk1003mike/Shutterstock.com; p. 7 (inset) wawritto/Shutterstock.com; p. 9 (oak tree) pzAxe/Shutterstock.com; p. 9 (acorn) 3523studio/Shutterstock.com; p. 10 ullstein bild/ Getty Images; p. 11 David Fettes/Shutterstock.com; p. 12 Ger Bosma/Getty Images; p. 13 Vitaly Ilyasov/ Shutterstock.com; p. 15 (shark) wildestanimal/Shutterstock.com; p. 15 (shark tooth) -/Stringer/AFP/Getty Images; p. 16 Dennis W. Donohue/Shutterstock.com; p. 17 Maryna Pleshkun/Shutterstock.com; p. 19 (grass) Alexander Mak/ Shutterstock.com; p. 19 (mouse) Tsekhmaster/Shutterstock.com; p. 19 (snake) kamnuan/Shutterstock.com; p. 19 (grasshopper) Photopen/Shutterstock.com; p. 19 (rabbit) Oleksandr Lytvynenko/Shutterstock.com; p. 19 (hawk) Keneva Photography/Shutterstock.com; p. 19 (lizard) Balakleypb/Shutterstock.com; p. 21 Jason Maehl/Getty Images; p. 21 (inset) William F. Campbell/The LIFE Images Collection/Getty Images; p. 22 Samuel Acosta/Shutterstock.com

Cataloging-in-Publication Data

Names: Pressberg, Dava.
Title: Producers, consumers, and decomposers / Dava Pressberg.
Description: New York : PowerKids Press, 2017. | Series: Spotlight on ecology and life science | Includes index.
Identifiers: ISBN 9781499426199 (pbk.) | ISBN 9781499425949 (library bound) | ISBN 9781499425925 (6 pack)
Subjects: LCSH: Biogeochemical cycles--Juvenile literature. | Biodegradation--Juvenile literature. | Ecology--Juvenile literature.
Classification: LCC QH344.P74 2017 | DDC 577.1--dc23

Manufactured in China

CPSIA Compliance Information: Batch #BW17PK For further information contact Rosen Publishing, New York, New York at 1-800-237-9932.

CONTENTS

CHAPTER ONE

WHAT'S ON THE MENU?

Each living thing on Earth is part of a food chain. A food chain describes the flow of energy and **nutrients** from one living thing to another. Food chains tell us which **organisms** are on the menu for other organisms.

This food chain diagram shows which organism eats which.

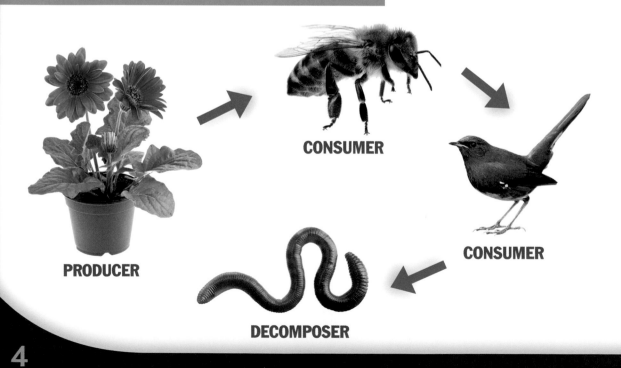

CONSUMER

CONSUMER

PRODUCER

DECOMPOSER

This honeybee relies on flowers for food. The flower is a producer. The bee is a consumer.

Different organisms play different roles, or parts, in the food chain. They're put into groups called trophic levels. The trophic levels include producers, consumers, and decomposers. Producers are autotrophs, which means they make their own food. They're the first level in the food chain. Some consumers eat the producers, making those consumers the second level. Some consumers eat other consumers. They make up the next levels of the food chain. Decomposers are the last level. Decomposers break down the nutrients in consumers and producers once the organisms in those groups die. Each trophic level is important to the food chain.

CHAPTER TWO

PRODUCING FOOD

Producers are the only living things in the food chain that are able to create their own food. Many of them do this through a process called photosynthesis. Plants are the most common autotrophs.

What do plants need to survive? They need sunlight, water, and a gas called carbon dioxide. Plants use these three ingredients to create food. Sunlight is the first ingredient— that's where almost all energy in the food chain begins. Plants take in sunlight through their leaves. The cells of the leaves contain **chlorophyll**, which catches the sunlight.

Sunlight **reacts** with carbon dioxide, which the plant takes from the air, and water, which is collected from the soil through the plant's roots. Through photosynthesis, these three ingredients create a kind of sugar and another gas called oxygen. People and animals need oxygen to live. In this way, plants benefit all other living creatures on Earth.

PHOTOSYNTHESIS

SUNLIGHT

OXYGEN O_2

CARBON DIOXIDE CO_2

WATER H_2O

Most plants start as seeds, which have enough nutrients to get the plant started. With enough water, the seed grows roots. It becomes a sprout with tiny leaves. Then it's ready to make its own food!

CHAPTER THREE

DIFFERENT KINDS OF PRODUCERS

There are around 400,000 species, or kinds, of plants on Earth that people have found and named. There are even more that haven't been discovered yet. Each of these producers has a specific role in its **ecosystem**.

Most plants produce flowers, fruits, or nuts. Many animals in the ecosystem eat these parts of the plant. For example, a crab apple tree produces small apples. These apples hold the seeds of the crab apple tree. When a deer eats a crab apple, the deer gets the nutrients from that fruit. The tree benefits because the deer may scatter the seeds so new crab apple trees can grow.

"Algae" is a term that refers to a large group of underwater producers. Some algae are huge seaweeds, while others are single-celled organisms. Even though they don't look like normal plants, they also go through photosynthesis to produce food for themselves. Many fish and **crustaceans** eat algae.

Oak trees produce acorns. Acorns provide nutrients for many consumers, such as squirrels, mice, deer, and woodpeckers.

CHAPTER FOUR

PRIMARY CONSUMERS

Primary consumers are animals that eat only producers. They are called herbivores. Animals that eat plants get the nutrients and energy they need to live and grow from them. Different animals enjoy different plants. All have adapted to the food they eat. For example, some birds have strong, cone-shaped beaks that can crack nuts. Other birds have long, thin beaks for picking up seeds. Deer and cattle have flat teeth for grinding up grasses.

Some of the largest dinosaurs survived on plants alone!

An African elephant can consume up to 300 pounds (136 kg) of food each day!

Primary consumers are sometimes very small. They can be insects, such as grasshoppers, which eat grasses. They might be larvae, or young bugs, such as caterpillars that eat leaves. Fruit bats are primary consumers that like to eat bananas, avocados, and mangoes.

Plant-based diets aren't just for small creatures, though. In fact, the largest land animal in the world is an herbivore. African elephants eat tree bark, leaves, grasses, roots, and fruit.

CHAPTER FIVE

SECONDARY CONSUMERS

Secondary consumers are the creatures that eat primary consumers. Animals that eat only meat are called carnivores. Some secondary consumers are omnivores because they eat both plants and animals. A good example of a secondary consumer is a wolf that eats a primary consumer, such as a deer.

This raccoon is a primary consumer when it eats fruit, but it is a secondary consumer when it eats fish that eat plants.

WARBLER AND CATERPILLAR

Secondary consumers are sometimes small creatures. Some birds, such as warblers, eat caterpillars. Most caterpillars feed on the leaves of trees, so they're primary consumers. Because it feeds on these caterpillars, the warbler is a secondary consumer. The warbler uses nutrients from caterpillars to **nourish** its body.

Some secondary consumers are huge. The blue whale is the largest animal in the world today. It eats a lot of krill, which are small shrimp-like creatures that live in the ocean. A blue whale can eat up to 4 tons (3.6 mt) of krill each day.

CHAPTER SIX

TOP OF THE FOOD CHAIN

Animals that eat secondary consumers are tertiary consumers. Consumers that have no natural predators are the apex predators in an ecosystem. Apex predators are at the top of the food chain.

A great white shark is at the top of its ocean food chain. These sharks like to eat seals. If the great white shark eats a seal that ate a fish that ate algae, then the shark is a tertiary consumer. The great white shark isn't usually **prey** for other animals, which makes it an apex predator.

Hawks are birds of prey. They are amazing predators that swoop out of the sky and catch many different animals in their claws. A hawk would be considered a tertiary consumer if it ate a snake that ate a mouse that ate seeds.

This is a tooth from the biggest type of shark that ever lived—the megalodon. This shark used to be at the top of the ocean's food chain.

This great white shark has hundreds of sharp teeth and amazing senses, as well as a body that can grow more than 20 feet (6 m) long.

CHAPTER SEVEN

DECOMPOSERS

Decomposers and scavengers may have the dirtiest jobs in the world. Scavengers are animals that eat dead animals, which are called carrion. Decomposers are organisms that break down dead plants and animals. Decomposers turn dead organisms into nutrients, such as nitrogen and carbon. Producers take these nutrients from the soil to grow. It all comes full circle!

Vultures are scavengers. They feed on the bodies of dead animals, or carrion.

Earthworms are one of the most well-known decomposers. They like to eat dead things. Their waste materials are called casts, and they're very rich in nutrients. They make the soil healthy.

Fungi, such as mold and mushrooms, are decomposers. They absorb nutrients from dead things as they break them down. Bacteria are other common decomposers. These creatures are so tiny you can't see them, but they are living on everything around you—including you! Some bacteria help us absorb nutrients into our bodies. Other bacteria return nutrients to the soil after an animal or plant has died. Some bacteria are helpful, while other bacteria are harmful.

CHAPTER EIGHT

FOOD WEBS

Food chains are simple. There's one line that connects a producer to one or more consumers. However, creatures usually eat more than one kind of food. When you imagine all the different food chains that can happen in an ecosystem, that's called a food web.

Like food chains, food webs show a **transfer** of energy between organisms. The energy from the sun helps all the plants in an ecosystem grow. Many primary consumers eat these plants, and many secondary consumers eat those primary consumers. In the same way, tertiary consumers will eat many different secondary consumers. While each food chain shows one possible path that nutrients and energy can take, a food web is closer to what actually happens in an ecosystem. Food webs show us that all animals in an ecosystem are connected.

GRASSLAND ECOSYSTEM FOOD WEB

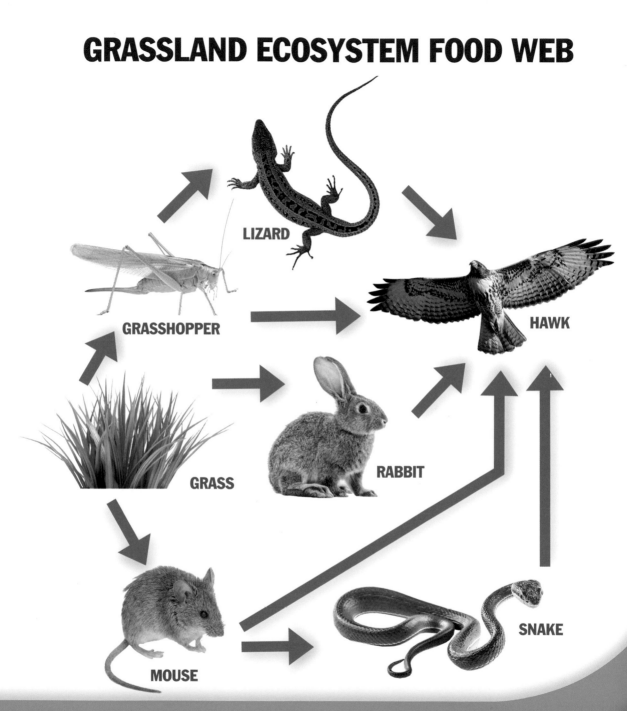

LIZARD

GRASSHOPPER

HAWK

GRASS

RABBIT

SNAKE

MOUSE

At the end of every food web, there are decomposers. They consume all of the plants and animals in this food web after they've died.

CHAPTER NINE

AN ECOSYSTEM IN BALANCE

It's important that an ecosystem is balanced. A balanced ecosystem has enough energy and nutrients available for each part of the food web.

Biomass is material that comes from both living and dead organisms. There is less biomass in each level of a healthy food web.

A food web is healthy if it's shaped like a **pyramid**. The producers are on the bottom, and they should represent the greatest biomass in the ecosystem. The next part of the pyramid is the primary consumers. As you move up the pyramid to the secondary and tertiary consumers, there should be less biomass in each section.

For example, there should be fewer lions than there are gazelles in a food web. If there are too many lions, the gazelle population will decrease too much and there won't be enough food to **sustain** the predators.

Doug Smith was the head scientist in charge of the Yellowstone Wolf Project. In this photograph, Smith and his team put a radio collar on a young wolf to keep track of it.

DOUG SMITH

Wolves were over-hunted in Yellowstone National Park until there were none left. With wolves gone, elk didn't have as many natural predators, which affected the ecosystem. When wolves were **reintroduced** again in 1995, the ecosystem completely changed again, and the food web is now healthier.

CHAPTER TEN

ALL CONNECTED

Each part of a food web is important. That means we must leave natural ecosystems the way they are. If one animal population suffers, the whole food web is affected.

Humans often **damage** the balance of natural ecosystems. In the past, animals such as gray wolves and whales were greatly overhunted—almost to **extinction**. People also cut down great amounts of trees, which animals depend on for food and shelter. Sometimes, people introduce harmful animals into an ecosystem. These animals are called invasive species. The introduction of the Burmese python to the Everglades has had a huge effect on the ecoystem there. People must follow and enforce laws against overhunting and introducing new animals.

Producers, consumers, and decomposers are necessary to every ecosystem. The food web shows how all living things in the world are connected. We all need each other to live!

BURMESE PYTHON

GLOSSARY

chlorophyll (KLOHR-uh-fihl) The green matter in plants that makes it possible for them to make food.

crustacean (kruhs-TAY-shun) An animal with a hard shell, jointed limbs, feelers, and no backbone.

damage (DAA-mihj) To cause harm.

ecosystem (EE-koh-sis-tuhm) A natural community of living and nonliving things.

extinction (ihk-STINK-shun) When all members of a species have died.

nourish (NUR-ish) To be provided with food and nutrients.

nutrient (NOO-tree-ehnt) Something taken in by a plant or animal that helps it grow and stay healthy.

organism (OHR-guh-nih-zuhm) A single living thing.

prey (PRAY) An animal hunted by other animals for food.

pyramid (PEER-uh-mihd) A shape or object that is wide near the bottom and narrows as it reaches the top.

react (ree-AKT) To change after coming into contact with another substance.

reintroduce (ree-ihn-truh-DOOS) To bring something back.

sustain (suh-STAYN) To provide what is needed for something to live.

transfer (TRANS-fuhr) The act or process of moving something from one place to another.

INDEX

PRIMARY SOURCE LIST

Page 10
Brachiosaurus skeleton. Fossilized skeleton. From the late Jurassic period. Now kept at the Museum of Natural History, Berlin, Germany.

Page 15 (inset)
Megalodon tooth. Fossilized bone. Found near Pokupsko, Croatia. 2015. Now kept at the Croatian Natural History Museum in Zagreb, Croatia.

Page 21 (inset)
Doug Smith and team put radio collar on gray wolf pup. Photograph. Taken by William F. Campbell. Taken at Yellowstone National Park. 1996.

WEBSITES